First published in 2004
by Wow Worldwide Ltd.
All rights reserved.
Text and illustrations copyright © 2004
Wow Worldwide Ltd.

A CIP catalogue record for this book is available from the British Library upon request.
ISBN   0-9547283-0-0

Series Editor
Kathy Robinson
Kathy Robinson is the founder of the "Signs for Success" programme
which uses sign language to raise levels of reading,
writing and spelling in young children.

Series Sign Consultant
Frances Elton - City University,London

Designed, Illustrated and Art Directed
Sam Williams, Andrew Crowson, Scott Gibson

Printed in China

First signing
ABC

Wow Worldwide Limited

How to get the most from your WOW first signing ABC book.

Sign with me now!
Just follow these simple instructions:

1. The Wow character is making the sign on every right-hand page. Say the word as you sign it.

2. Make the sound of the letter as you fingerspell it.

3. Point to the graphic image (e.g. 'alligator').

4. Make the sound of each letter as you fingerspell the word on each page.

5. Say the word again.

a

alligator

b

book

C

cat

d

d o g

e

elephant

f

fish

g

gate

h

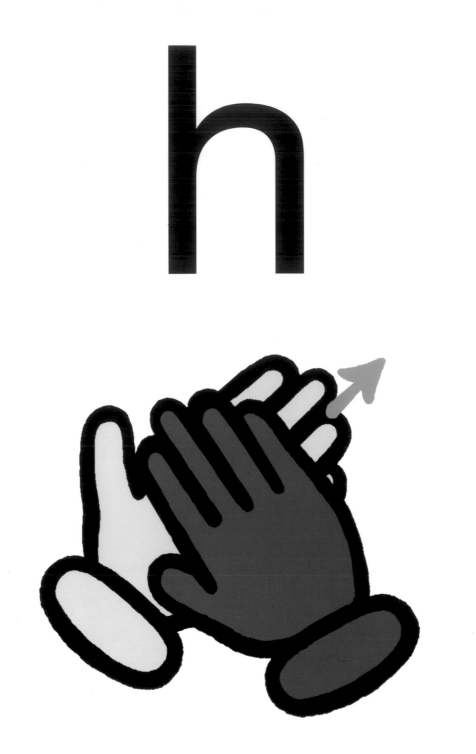

house

i

insect

j

jelly

k

key

l

lion

m

monkey

n

night

O

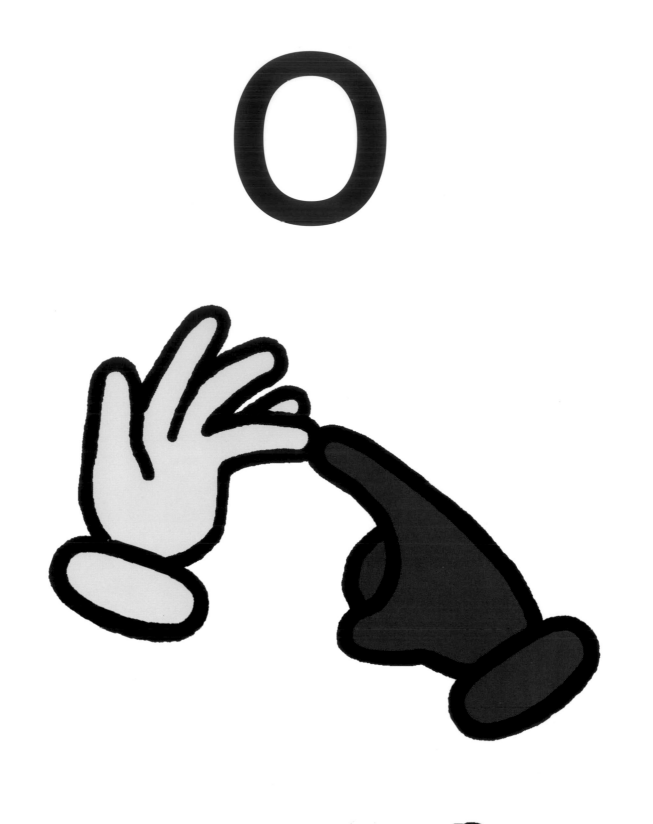

orange

p

pizza

q

queen

r

rainbow

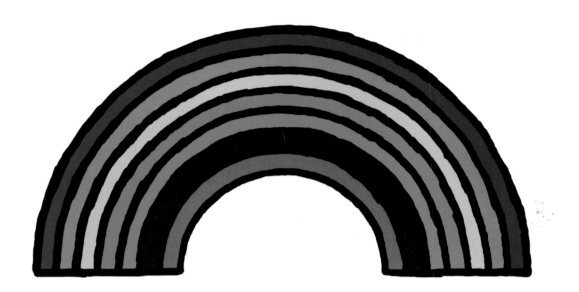

S

s u n

t

truck

u

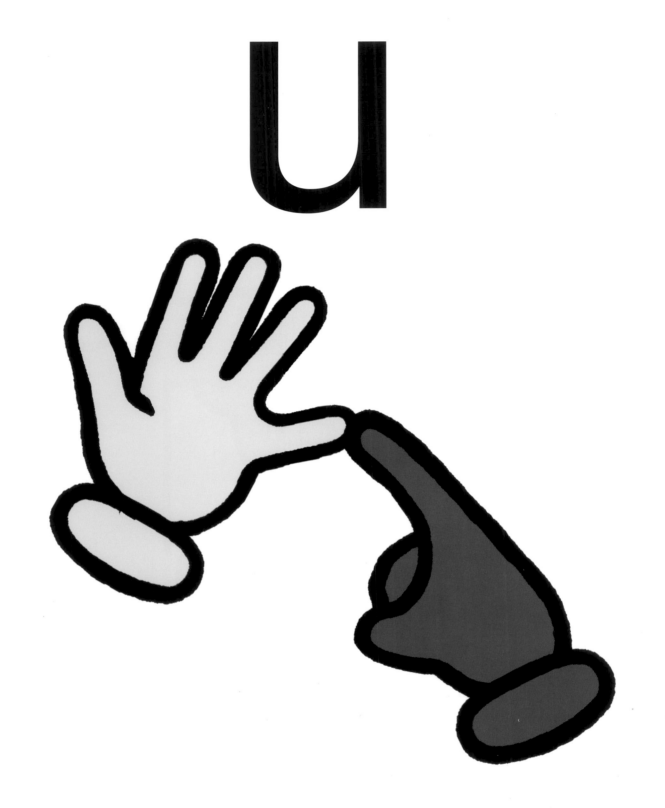

umbrella

V

van

W

worm

X

b o x

y

yellow

z

zip

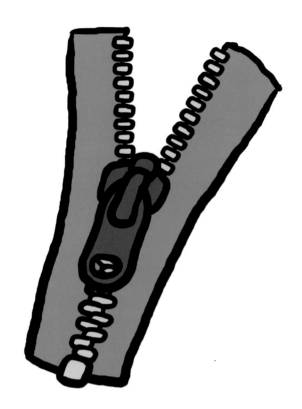

WOW™
You're doing great!
For more fingerspelling and signing fun and useful information go to www.wowworldwide.co.uk

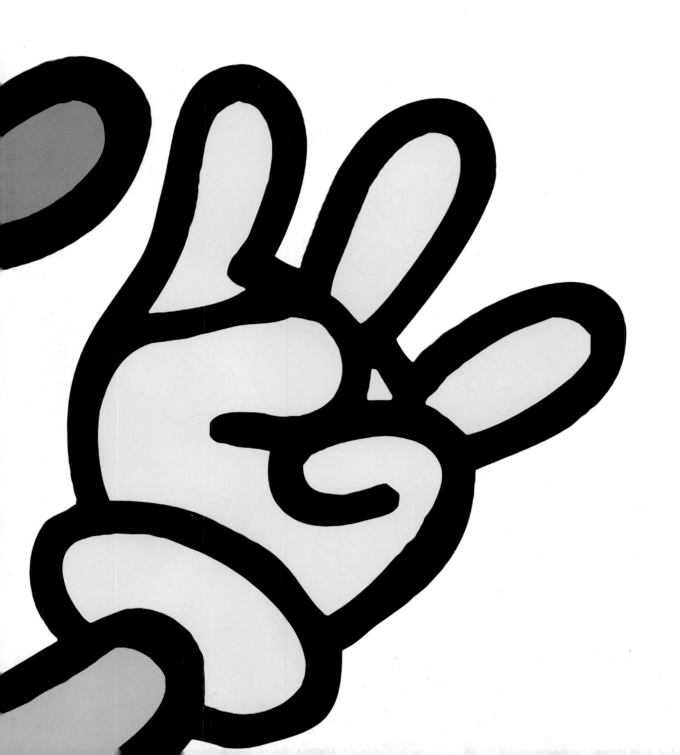